THE KIDS CAN DO IT BOOK

BY
DERI ROBINS, MEG SANDERS, AND KATE CROCKER

ILLUSTRATED BY
CHARLOTTE STOWELL

Kingfisher Books

NEW YORK

CONTENTS

KINGFISHER BOOKS
Grisewood & Dempsey Inc.
95 Madison Avenue, New York, New York 10016
First American edition 1993
Copyright © Grisewood & Dempsey Ltd. 1989, 1990, 1993
All rights reserved under Pan-American and International Copyright Conventions
Library of Congress Cataloging-in-Publication Data
Robins, Deri
The kids can do it book: fun things to make and do.
Presents indoor and outdoor activities including cooking,
disguises, dice games, picnics, and balloon fun.
1. Creative activities and seat work – Juvenile literature.
2. Handicraft – Juvenile literature.
[1. Handicraft. 2. Games. 3. Cookery.] I. Sanders, Meg
II. Crocker, Kate. III. Stowell, Charlotte, ill.
IV. Title.
GV1203.R5718 1993   790.1'922   92-43345
ISBN 1-85697-860-5
Cover design by The Pinpoint Design Company
Printed in Spain

Making Things

Playing Games

Cooking Treats

This book is packed with fun things to do!
The symbols on the left show you the different
kinds of activity you will find.

Remember, although most of these activities are
easily done on your own, sometimes you will need
the help of an adult. Take special care with
knives and scissors and ask an adult to help you
when cooking with heat.

A is for acrobat

To make this colorful acrobat, you will need:

    Some tracing paper
    Cardboard
    Crayons or paints
    Scissors
    Four fasteners
    A popsicle stick
    Tape

1. Trace arms, legs, and body onto cardboard. Color them, cut out carefully, and make holes—use a hole punch if possible.

2. Attach the arms and legs to the body with the fasteners, so that they move easily. Now tape the stick to the back of the acrobat.

Tape stick to back.

When you've made an acrobat, try making other circus figures, such as a dancer, or a clown using the same basic five shapes.

Shake the stick up and down, and from side to side—and watch the acrobat perform his dance!

RIGHT LEG

LEFT LEG

BODY

RIGHT ARM

LEFT ARM

5

. . . animal alphabet

The animal world is full of things that slither and crawl . . .

. . . things that climb . . .

. . . things that fly . . .

. . . things that swim . . .

. . . things that squeak . . . and roar!

Collect as many animal pictures as you can. Cut them out of magazines, or draw them yourself. Try to find an animal for every letter in the alphabet, and paste them into a scrapbook.

You could even make up your own story using your animal pictures. Try to think of names beginning with the same letter as each of your alphabet animals. Here are some to get you started: Albert Ape, Boris Bear, Calvin Cat, Daisy Dog—the rest are up to you!

. . . and animals

One very nice thing about being outdoors is that you are never alone! Even the smallest backyard is teeming with animal life.

If you keep a caterpillar in a jar like this, you will gradually see an amazing change. After several weeks, it will spin a silky case called a cocoon around its body. Finally, the cocoon will open and a shimmering butterfly will appear. Let the butterfly fly away outside.

Paper top with air holes

Feed them fresh leaves (the type you found them on) each day.

Birds are always grateful for scraps of bread, bacon, and nuts, especially in winter when food is scarce. Put some water out, too.

Fresh pond weed

Stones for frogs to climb onto

If there's a pond near your home, collect some frog spawn in the spring and keep it in a glass tank. Watch as the spawn turns into tadpoles, and then into frogs.

Always ask an adult to go with you when you visit a pond, or river, and make sure you return your baby frogs to the water as soon as possible.

B is for balloons

Have you ever tried filling a balloon with water instead of air? The balloon should be less than half full, and the neck should be tied tightly. Use it as a ball — and be prepared to get wet if you drop it!

How long can you keep an air-filled balloon off the ground just by blowing it? And have you ever tried to burst someone else's balloon *without* using your hands?

A squishy game of catch

Keep it up!

Tie balloons around your waist with string.

1. Mix the dough well with your hands.

2. On a floured surface, roll out until quarter of an inch (5 mm) thick.

3. Cut out bear shapes with a knife. Knead the trimmings together and roll out again to make more bears.

4. Bake at 350° F for 10-15 minutes and leave to cool. Decorate with confectioner's sugar mixed with a little water.

. . . bear

To make these gingerbread teddy bears, you will need:

    ½ cup soft brown sugar
    ⅓ cup margarine
    4 tablespoons corn syrup
    1½ cups flour
    1½ teaspoons ground ginger

Melt the margarine, sugar, and syrup in a pan over a low heat. Stir in the flour and ginger. Now follow the pictures to make your bears.

. . . and bubbles

To make really giant bubbles, you will need:
    About 15 inches thin wire
    A bottle of bubble-blowing liquid
    2 tablespoons glycerine
    2 tablespoons dishwashing liquid
Ask an adult to bend the wire into a giant
loop, like the one shown here. Mix all your
ingredients in a shallow bowl, and gently
dip your giant loop in and out of the liquid.
Don't blow—just wave the loop around in
the air to make megabubbles!

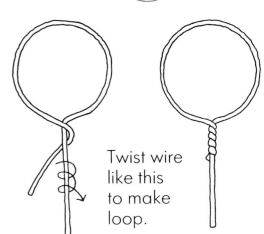

Twist wire
like this
to make
loop.

10

C is for chocolate

Cooking with chocolate is always special! You will need an adult's help with these two recipes.

CHOCOLATE ICE CREAM CUPS

6 oz. (120g) chocolate Ice cream
5 dried apricots 10 almonds

Melt the chocolate in an ovenproof bowl over a pan of hot water. Chop up the apricots and almonds, and add to the chocolate.

  Use the mixture to line paper baking cups, and leave to set in the refrigerator. Later, top up with ice cream, and serve at once!

CHOCOLATE FUDGE

6oz. (120g) chocolate
¼ cup butter
2 tablespoons milk
1lb. (500g) confectioner's sugar
¼ teaspoon vanilla extract

Melt chocolate and butter in an ovenproof bowl over a pan of hot water. Take off the heat and stir in milk, sugar, and vanilla extract. Spoon mixture into a shallow pan, and leave somewhere cool to set.

. . . coolers

Here are some ideas for staying
COOL when the weather is HOT!
You will need some fruit juice, empty
yogurt containers, and popsicle sticks.

1. Pour the fruit juice into the yogurt
containers, and put into the freezer.

2. When the juice has started to freeze, push a
popsicle stick into the middle of each container.
Return to the freezer until frozen. Then pull
them out!

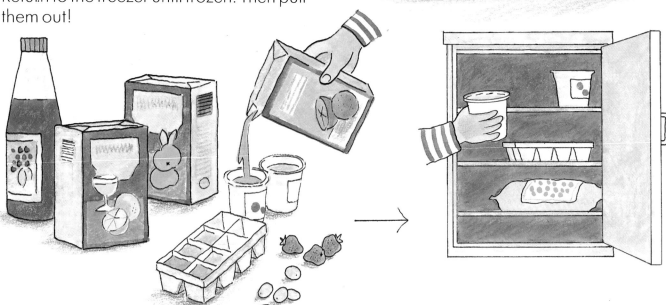

3. Make colored ice cubes out of fruit juice. A
grape or strawberry in each looks pretty.

If you let each
layer freeze at a
time, you can
make multi-
colored
popsicles
from different
juices.

12

. . . and crocodile

For this quick and colortul candy, all you will need is some almond paste and some red or green food coloring.

1. Take a piece of almond paste, add a few drops of the food coloring and mix in well with your hands.

2. Roll some of the almond paste into sausage shapes, and flatten out one end to make the tails. Make little legs and stick them to the body by smoothing the edges of the paste with the flat side of a knife.

Score backs with fork.

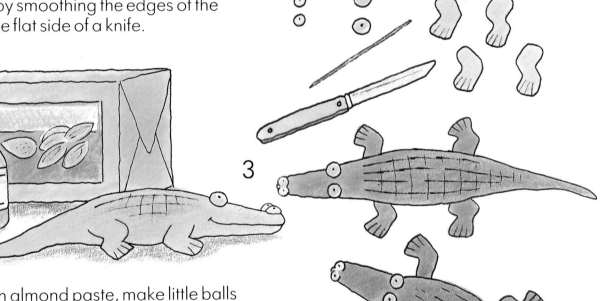

3. Using plain almond paste, make little balls for eyes and snout, and stick on with a tiny blob of jam.

D is for dinosaur

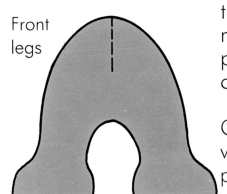

This is a Stegosaurus — one of the dinosaurs that lived on earth millions of years ago. To make the model, you will need some tracing paper, cardboard, scissors, and bright paints or pencils.

Trace the three outlines onto cardboard. Color both sides brightly, and cut out. Cut slits where shown, and simply slot the legs into place.

Front legs

Back legs

Body

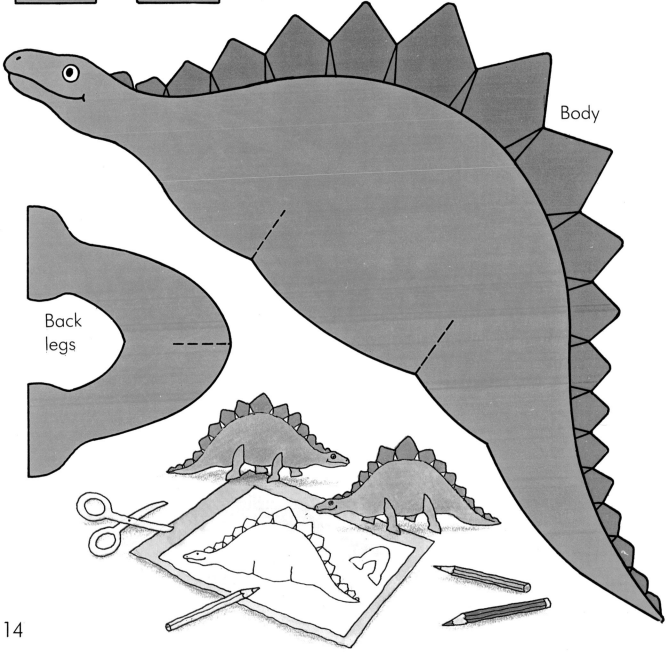

14

. . . disguise

Amaze your family and friends with these foolproof disguises!

FALSE GLASSES AND NOSE
You will need five pipe cleaners, scissors, glue, and thin cardboard.

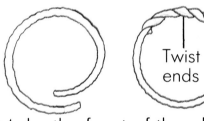

Twist ends

Bend in half and twist.

1. Make the front of the glasses from three pipe cleaners, as shown above.

2. Trace the rims onto cardboard, and cut out.

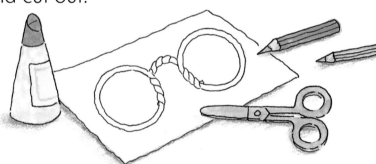

Nose

3. Color the circles to look like eyes, and make holes in the middle. Use the last two pipe cleaners to make the "arms" of the glasses. Bend the ends to fit around your ears. Now glue the eyes in the frames.

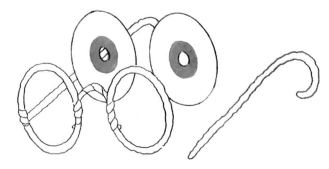

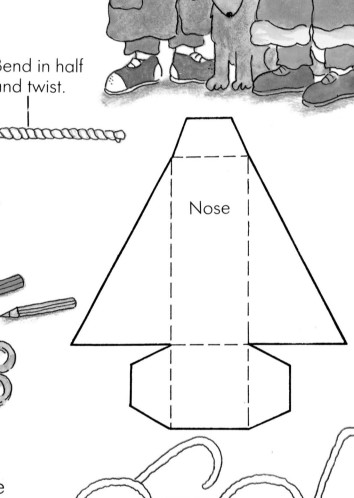

4. Finally, to make the nose, trace the shape shown on cardboard. Paint it to match your skin, fold it, and glue it on the glasses.

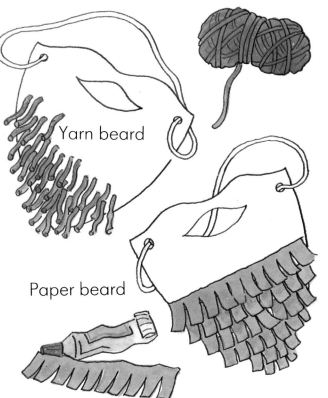

Yarn beard

Paper beard

A BEARD
Cut a beard shape out of cardboard to fit your face. Cut a hole for your mouth.

Spread some glue on the cardboard, and glue on pieces of yarn or strips of paper cut into fringes. When the glue has dried, make a small hole at each side and thread some elastic through.

A wig

BALD HEAD
Give yourself a bald head by tucking all your hair into a plain swimming cap, as close to your skin color as possible.

For a wig, cover the cap with glue and pieces of yarn or paper.

MAKE-UP
Ask if you can borrow an adult's make-up for your disguise.

Blot out your eyebrows with foundation and powder, and draw in a new shape with an eyebrow pencil. Eyebrow pencils are also good for adding wrinkles, moles, and scars!

. . . and dunking

Make sure you are wearing old clothes when you play this dunking game!

Fill a bucket or bowl with water, and float some apples on top. Now see if you can get an apple out — *without* using your hands!

Or, tie the apples to a line with strong thread. Keep your hands behind your back as you try to bite the apples.

E is for eggs

Make breakfast-time fun by turning your hard-boiled eggs into funny animals or creatures from outer space! If you want to eat the egg, make sure you use non-toxic pens, as some of the color may stain the egg inside.

For colorful eggs, try boiling white or pale-brown eggs for 10–15 minutes in water colored with a few drops of food coloring.

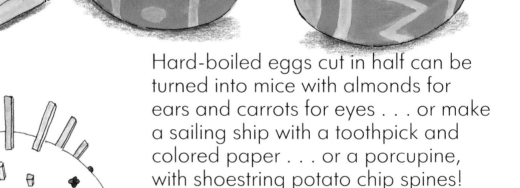

Hard-boiled eggs cut in half can be turned into mice with almonds for ears and carrots for eyes . . . or make a sailing ship with a toothpick and colored paper . . . or a porcupine, with shoestring potato chip spines!

Decorate eggs with initials or names for a party!

18

. . . elephant

If you trace this elephant onto thin cardboard and cut it out, you can use it to draw around again and again.

Make lots of elephants, and color them with bright paints or pencils. Hang one elephant up by its tail with a thumbtack, and hook the rest on by their tails and trunks.

First trace the elephant.

Some can have trunks pointing up, and some pointing down.

19

. . . and engine

You will need two large cardboard boxes for the engine, and one for each of the cars. You will also need some bright poster paints, some paper plates, and children's glue.

Glue the boxes together, with the open sides facing up—except for the engine which should have the open end facing backward.

Paint the engine in bright colors. When the paint has dried, glue on paper plates to make the wheels and the engine's face. Roll up pieces of cardboard into tubes to make the buffers and smokestack.

Paint boxes brightly.

Cut off flaps

Cut out

Flap

Stick on wheel.

Why not make a roll of tickets? Draw them onto a long, narrow strip of paper, and wind them around an empty cardboard roll. Wear this around your neck on a long piece of string. Or you could make a ticket office from another cardboard box.

Tickets, please!

F is for fair

Invite all your friends and their families to a wonderful fair in your yard! (You'll need lots of friends to run the booths, too.) You could charge a small fee for each of the games, and have little prizes for the winners. Rummage sales are always fun—your old junk might seem amazingly interesting to someone else!

Fortune teller with "crystal ball" (goldfish bowl).

Ring toss — cut rings from cardboard, and see how many you can throw over a stick.

Rummage sales are always popular!

Put on a show! The puppets are just socks with buttons sewn on for eyes, and little ears made from pieces of felt.

Bowling alley

Old plastic bottles

Refreshment stand

Score 10 points with 3 balls to win.

Cut holes from an old box for a marble arcade.

23

. . . and farm

Ask an adult to give you three large empty matchboxes, and two small ones. You will need some thin cardboard, tracing paper, glue, and paints. Using a ruler, trace the outlines and dotted lines onto cardboard. You can paint them later, when they have been put together.

FARMHOUSE

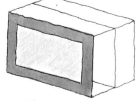

1. Glue both parts of a large matchbox together.

2. Trace the farmhouse onto cardboard. Fold along the dotted lines, cut the slits in the roof and glue to the matchbox.

3. Trace two chimneys, and slot into the roof.

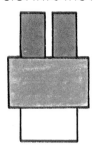

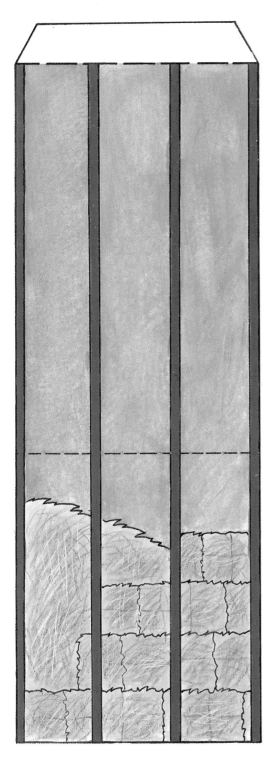

BARN

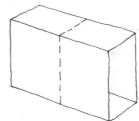

1. Cut the open end of a large matchbox in half.

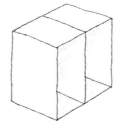

2. Glue the halves together like this.

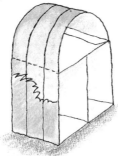

3. Trace the barn shape onto cardboard, cut out and glue to the matchbox like this.

4. Fill with hay.

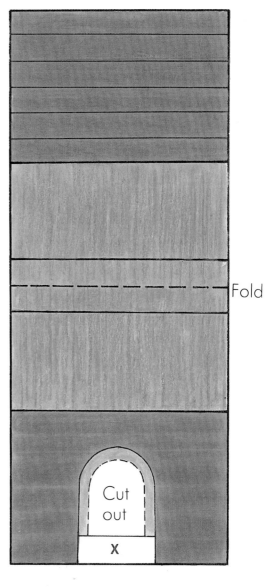

Fold

Cut out

X

X

HENHOUSE

Glue two small matchboxes together. Trace the henhouse shape, cut out, and glue onto matchboxes as shown. Push four toothpicks into the base of the henhouse to make stilts. Trace the ramp onto card, and glue this onto the front.

Glue ramp here.

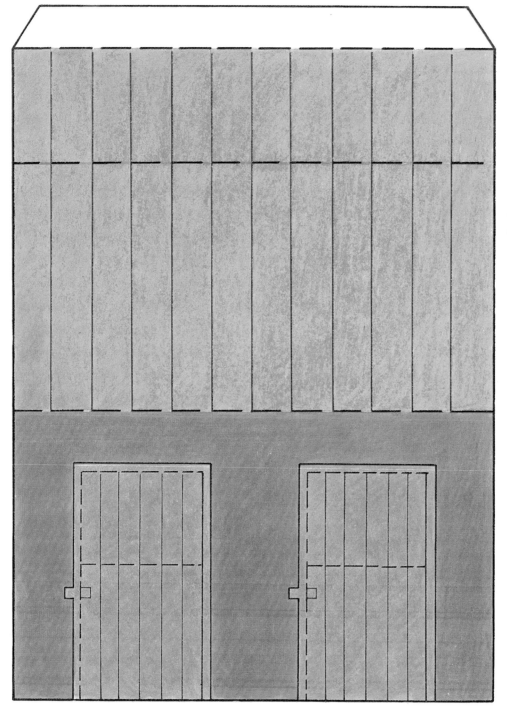

1. Glue both parts of a large matchbox together.

2. Trace the stable outline onto cardboard, cut it out and glue onto the matchbox.

3. Cut the dotted lines around the doors, so that they open in two parts.

4. Put a horse (page 27) in the stable.

BUNDLES OF HAY FOR STABLE AND BARN
Gather some dry grass from the yard, and tie into little bundles with yarn. Feed it to the horse in the stable, and store the bales in the barn.

DUCK POND
Use blue and green paper, or color with paints. You will also need a small lid from a jar.

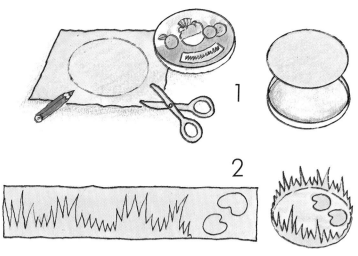

1. Draw around the lid, and cut out a blue circle. Stick this into the lid.

2. Draw shapes like these onto green paper, and cut out. Glue on to make weeds and lilypads.

HENS AND DUCKS
Use colored modeling clay to make ducks and ducklings for the pond, and hens for the henhouse.

OTHER ANIMALS
Pipe cleaners can be twisted into all kinds of animal shapes. Here are three to start you off.

Follow the little pictures carefully. As well as pipe cleaners, you will need some absorbent cotton for the sheep, and some wool for the horse. The horse is tethered to a toothpick stuck in modeling clay.

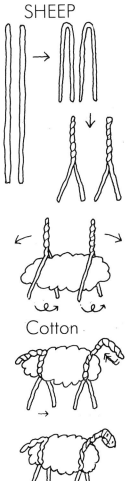

SHEEP

Cotton

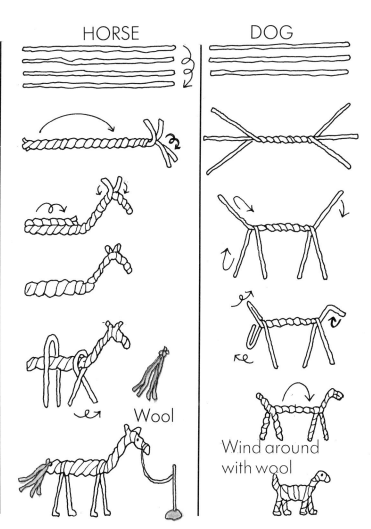

HORSE

Wool

DOG

Wind around with wool

G is for garden

Ask if you can have a garden plot to grow things in, and try planting these easy flowers.

Sow sunflower seeds in a sunny flowerbed in the spring. As they start to grow, tie them to stakes or to a fence to support their heavy heads. After the sunflowers have died, you can eat the seeds!

Nasturtiums are also easy to grow. Scatter the seeds evenly over a freshly-dug flowerbed or in a large tub or pot in spring. Cover with a fine layer of soil, and sprinkle regularly with water.

Sunflowers

Nasturtiums

28

. . . gift box

Put candy or little presents in these pretty gift boxes. To make them, you will need: thin cardboard (paint it first, or print with potatoes—see page 74), scissors and glue.

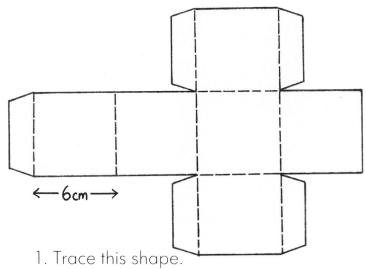

←6cm→

1. Trace this shape.

⭐ Ask an adult to help you copy the shape shown left onto cardboard. Use a pencil and ruler, and make each square 2½ x 2½ inches (6 x 6 cm). Cut it out—don't forget the flaps!

⭐ Fold up into a box shape, and glue the four side flaps inside the box. The top flap tucks in to close the box.

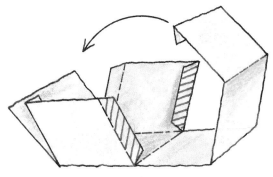

2. Fold up box.

3. Trace and glue to box.

⭐ Decorate your boxes—you could use glitter, or scraps of ribbon and lace. Or trace the little shapes shown left onto cardboard, paint, and cut out. Fold slightly along the middle lines, and glue to the box.

. . . and giraffe

Make this jungle jigsaw for yourself, or as a present.

1. Trace the giraffe onto a piece of cardboard. Draw in all the black lines, and put a faint pencil mark on all the patches that should be bright orange.

1

Paint a shoebox in giraffe colors, and keep the pieces in this.

2

2. Cut along all the lines to make a jigsaw. Paint all the marked pieces in orange, and the rest in bright yellow. Allow to dry.

H is for hideaway

Whatever the weather, it's always fun to make a secret hideaway! Spread blankets over chairs, clothes drying racks, or stepladders. Old cardboard boxes with the ends cut out make good doors and windows.

Hideaways are good for those quiet moments when you want to be alone. But you could also think about inviting some special friends **over** for a party!

. . . hippo

The hippopotamus is very fond of water! It spends its days pleasantly in the river, standing on the bottom with its head poking up above the surface.

To make this hippo dessert, you will need a can of pears, some lime gelatin, chocolate chips, and almonds or green candy.

1. Make the gelatin according to directions on package. Pour into shallow dishes and allow to set.

2. When the gelatin is set, arrange the pear halves on top. Give them chocolate eyes and noses, and almond or candy ears.

Chocolate chips stuck on with jam for eyes

Almonds or green candy pushed in for ears

. . . and hopscotch

Mark squares like the ones below with chalk—either on the sidewalk or in the playground.

Throw a small stone onto number 1 to start. Hop on one foot to number 1, pick up the stone, then hopscotch all the way to 12 and back again. After everyone has had a turn, throw the stone to number 2, and so on.

If you land on a line, or the stone misses a square, you must lose a turn.

I is for islands

This is a "catch" game for three or more players. One player is "it," and is known as the crocodile. Cut out and paint a cardboard mask for the crocodile to wear.

Make some "islands" out of painted cardboard pieces. These are the safe areas. The idea of the game is to run from island to island without being caught by the crocodile.

Only one person is allowed on any island at one time — if the crocodile catches you in between then you must change places.

1. Cut out the sides of a cardboard box.

2. Draw an island shape on each of the sides.

3. Cut out the islands, and paint them.

J is for jelly doughnut

Try these sticky eating games!

Eat a jelly doughnut from a plate without using your hands. (This is difficult.)

Feed a jelly doughnut to a friend while you are both blindfolded. (This is *very* difficult.)

Eat a jelly doughnut without once licking your lips. (This is almost impossible!)

. . . and jungle

To play this game you will need a die and a colored button for each player. Take turns throwing the die, and move the number thrown along the jungle track. On the way, follow these instructions:

START

If you land on a monkey's hand or foot, move forward so that you are on its tail.

 If you land on a butterfly, take a free turn.

If you land on a snake's head, slither back down to the end of its tail.

If you land on a beetle, lose a turn.

The winner is the first to reach the FINISH square.

FINISH

K is for king

Here's how to make a king's crown—either as a special paper hat, or for a party costume. You'll need some thin cardboard, paints, colored paper, scissors, and glue.

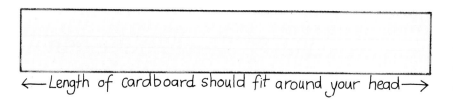

←—Length of cardboard should fit around your head—→

1. Cut the cardboard into a strip about 5 inches (12 cm) wide, and long enough to go around your head.

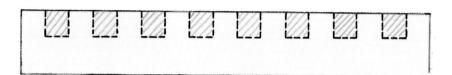

2. Copy the pattern shown here, and cut out the shaded areas. Bend into a circle, and glue or staple the edges.

This extra strip of cardboard will make your crown stronger.

3. Paint the crown with yellow or gold paint. Glue on "jewels" (colored paper or candy wrappers), and make a "fur" brim by gluing on some absorbent cotton.

. . . kite

To make this little kite, you will need a piece of thin cardboard measuring 12 inches (30 cm) square. You will also need a roll of masking tape, a spool of nylon thread, a needle, scissors, and some paper squares.

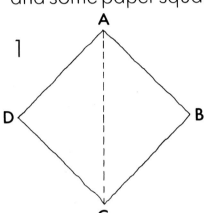

1

Fold the piece of cardboard in half from corner to corner and open it out again (1).

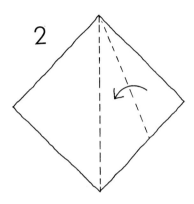

2

Fold the side AB into the center crease (2).

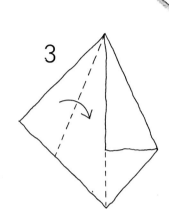

3

Now do the same with the side AD (3).

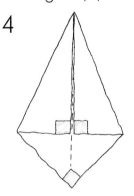

4

Cut some pieces of masking tape, and wrap them around corners B, C, and D to make them strong (4).

Cut a piece of thread 16 inches (40 cm) long, and thread the needle. Push the needle through corner C, and knot a loop.

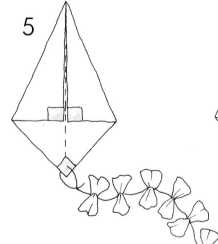

5

Starting at the top, tie the thread around the paper squares, to make bows all down the tail (5).

Thread the needle with the loose end of the thread

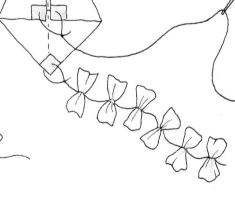

6

left on the spool. Sew through corners B and D, and knot the loose end. This is your kite string (6).

39

7

Paint a happy face or a bright pattern on your kite (7). Take it out to fly on a breezy day. The best places are fields or hills — somewhere well away from overhead wires or trees.

. . . and Kool 'n' Krazy

Just think of the best ice cream in the world—then double it! Try some of the ideas given here, or invent your own.

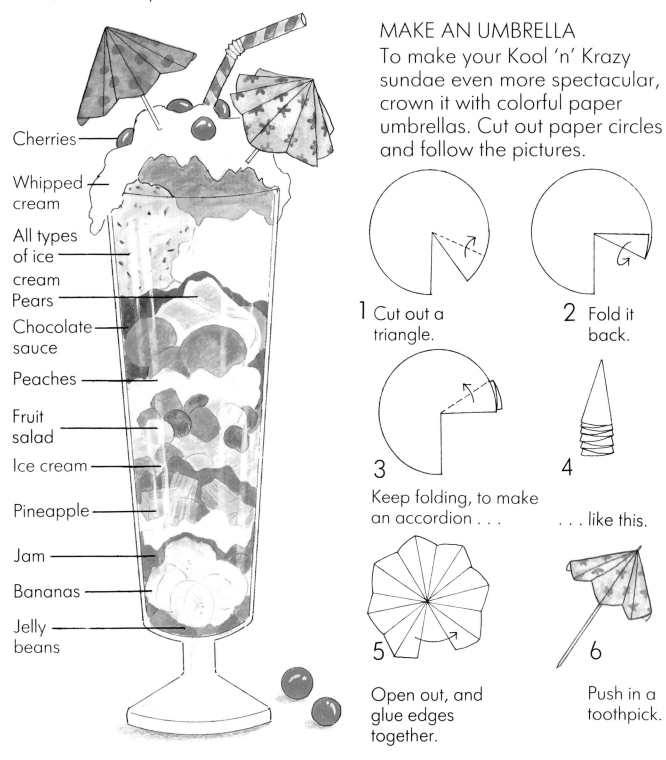

Cherries

Whipped cream

All types of ice cream

Pears

Chocolate sauce

Peaches

Fruit salad

Ice cream

Pineapple

Jam

Bananas

Jelly beans

MAKE AN UMBRELLA
To make your Kool 'n' Krazy sundae even more spectacular, crown it with colorful paper umbrellas. Cut out paper circles and follow the pictures.

1 Cut out a triangle.

2 Fold it back.

3 Keep folding, to make an accordion . . .

4 . . . like this.

5 Open out, and glue edges together.

6 Push in a toothpick.

L is for lantern

These look pretty for Christmas or Halloween. You will need: some colored paper or wrapping paper (each piece 4 x 6 inches (10 x 14 cm)), scissors, glue, tape, and thread.

1. Fold the paper in half.

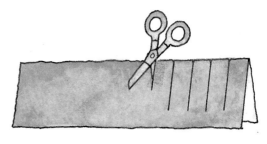

2. Make cuts along the folded edge.

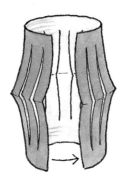

3. Open out, and glue the side edges together.

4. Glue on a paper strip to make a handle.

5. Draw and cut out a candle. Tape one end of a piece of thread to the candle, and tape the other end to the handle.

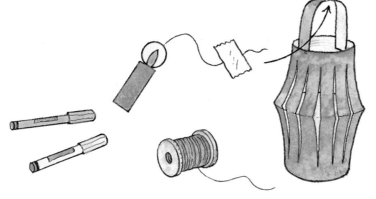

. . . and leapfrog

Once your tadpoles have turned into frogs (page 7) they'll be leaping all over the place. You can beat them at their own game with a little practice! How many different leapfrog games can you think up? Here are some to start you off.

Leapfrog using only one hand.

Leapfrog over someone on all fours.

Clap your hands once — or twice — before you land.

M is for mailbox

Special family occasions need a special mailbox. You will need one big cardboard box and one small one; paints and glue.

Slot

1

2

3

Flap

1. Fold the flaps of the big box together.

2. Cut a hole slightly smaller than the opening of the small box.

3. Glue the flaps of the small box onto the big one. Cut a slot in the top, and a flap at the bottom. Paint in a bright color.

. . . modeling

First of all, you have to make the modeling dough.
You will need:
4 cups of flour
1 cup of salt
2 tablespoons of cooking oil
1 ½ cups of water
Food coloring
Now follow the pictures.

1. Mix flour and salt, and gradually add the cooking oil and then the water until the mixture is smooth.

2. Knead the dough into a ball.

3. Color the dough with food coloring, and knead well.

4. Put in a plastic bag, and leave in the refrigerator for an hour.

There are dozens of things you can make with dough!

. . . and mouse

Odd socks love being turned into mice! All you need to do is to stuff the sock with pieces of crumpled newspaper, and tie yarn around the open end to look like a tail.

Glue on buttons for eyes and nose—or sew them to the sock before you stuff it. Make ears from felt, and sew them on, too.

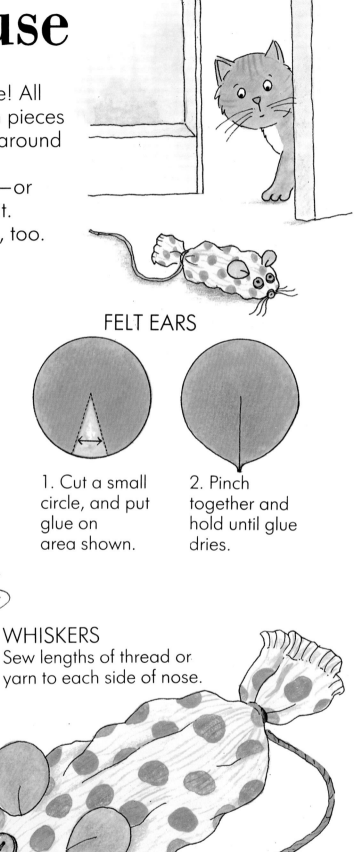

FELT EARS

1. Cut a small circle, and put glue on area shown.

2. Pinch together and hold until glue dries.

WHISKERS
Sew lengths of thread or yarn to each side of nose.

N is for newspaper

There are no end of things you can make with an old newspaper! Here are just a few ideas.

PAPER HAT
Fold up a sheet of newspaper as shown in the pictures below, and paint brightly for a party— or make a black witch's hat—or even a pirate's hat with a skull and crossbones!

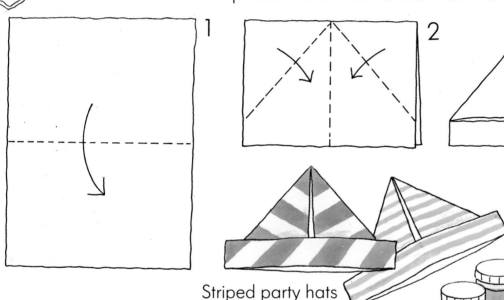

Striped party hats

MAGIC TREE
1. Roll up a sheet of newspaper fairly tightly. Slip one rubber band around the middle, and one around the bottom.

2. Now make four downward cuts, cutting as far as the first rubber band.

3. Pull the middle of the roll up gently to make a paper tree.

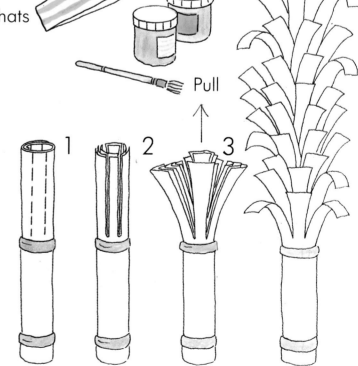

Pull

PAPIER-MÂCHÉ

1. Put 1 cup of flour in a mixing bowl. Measure out 1 cup of water, and add it to the flour gradually to make a paste.

2. Cover the outside of a bowl with petroleum jelly. Tear up newspaper into tiny strips, dip them into the paste, and stick several layers around the bowl.

3. When all the layers are quite dry, ease the papier-mâché off the bowl. Trim off any uneven bits, paint brightly, and varnish to give it a hard coat.

Once you've mastered the method, try to think up some papier-mâché ideas of your own!

These bowls have been turned into masks and decorations.

48

. . . and nonsense

Two or more players can play this drawing game.

Give each player a piece of paper and some colored pencils. Tell them to draw an animal head near the top of the sheet, and fold back the page so just the tip of the neck is showing.

Now pass the folded page to the next player, and draw the top half of an animal's body. Keep folding and passing it on until the bottom half and the legs have been drawn.

Open it up, and see what nonsense animals you have drawn!

O is for ostrich

This greeting card is very special. To make it, you will need some thick paper or thin cardboard, glue, paints, and scissors.

1. Cut two pieces of cardboard the same size. Fold one in half, and cut a slit near the middle.

2. Fold back the corners made by the slit.

3. Tuck the folded corners inside the folded cardboard.

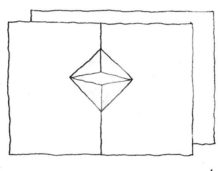

1

2

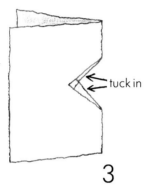

tuck in

3

4

5

4. Turn it over, and glue it onto the second piece of cardboard. Don't put glue on the back of the "beak."

5. When the glue is dry, paint the inside and outside of the card like the pictures shown below.

See the ostrich open its beak as the card opens!

50

. . . and outdoor art

Make life-sized pictures of your friends! Draw around them when they're lying down on a huge piece of paper. You can paint in the details later. Try painting with your fingers, or making bright footprints with your feet. Potatoes make good printers, too. Cut one in half, and draw a simple shape on the cut surface. Carefully cut away the surrounding flesh with a knife (not too sharp), and use the raised surface to print, using poster paints.

Self-portrait

Bright poster paints

Finger painting

Making footprint pictures

Draw around a friend

Potato prints

51

P is for picnic

Here are some delicious ideas for an outdoor feast on a sunny day.

PINK DRINK
Mix cranberry juice with lemonade.

DOUBLE-DECKER SANDWICHES
are made from three slices of bread and two layers of filling. Add potato chips for a crunchy bite.

WORMS IN SUNGLASSES
Use a dab of peanut butter to stick chocolate chips onto small pretzel logs.

PINWHEEL SANDWICHES
Cut the crusts off sliced bread, spread with a creamy filling like peanut butter, and roll up! The rolls can be cut into slices like a jelly roll cake.

CREAMY DIP
A tasty dip for raw vegetables and crackers — mix cream cheese with yogurt and chopped chives.

PICTURE SANDWICHES
Spread each slice of bread with butter, and use cold meats, salad stuff, peanuts, and slices of egg to make funny faces or little scenes.

CRUNCHY CAKES—Ask an adult to help you. Break a big bar of chocolate into squares. Put in a heatproof bowl and place in a pan of simmering shallow water to melt the chocolate. Stir in crunchy cereal and raisins, and put to set in cupcake cases or a cake pan.

ANTS ON A LOG
Mix three tablespoons of peanut butter with three tablespoons of cream cheese. Use this to fill the hollows of some sticks of celery. Dot with raisins.

ORANGE GELATIN
Cut six oranges in half, and carefully scoop out the flesh. Squeeze out as much juice as you can, and fill with water to make a pint of liquid. Use a little boiling water to melt a packet of orange gelatin, and add the orange water. Pour into each orange half, and allow to set. Serve by cutting into quarters.

. . . and pig

A mosaic is a picture made from little pieces of colored stone or paper glued together.

To make this mosaic pig, you will need some old magazines, scissors, and glue. Trace or copy the pig onto a sheet of cardboard before you begin.

Look through the magazines to find piglike colors — anything pink or red will do. Tear these pages into little pieces, about an inch across. Glue them all over the pig, overlapping them so that there are no white spaces left. When you have finished, trim the edges and draw on a piggy face.

Q is for quail

. . . and also for quoits! Quoits is a game in which the players throw rings over numbered objects to score points. To make a set of quail quoits, you will need six empty cardboard rolls, some thin cardboard, tracing paper, scissors, glue, and poster paints.

1. Trace the quail face onto cardboard, and cut out. Draw around the shape five more times, and paint all six faces. Paint the cardboard rolls, and stick on the quail faces when dry. Now make three cardboard rings like the one shown here.

2. Number the quails from 1 to 6, and stand them in a triangle. Now take turns to throw the rings over the quails. Who is the first to score 30?

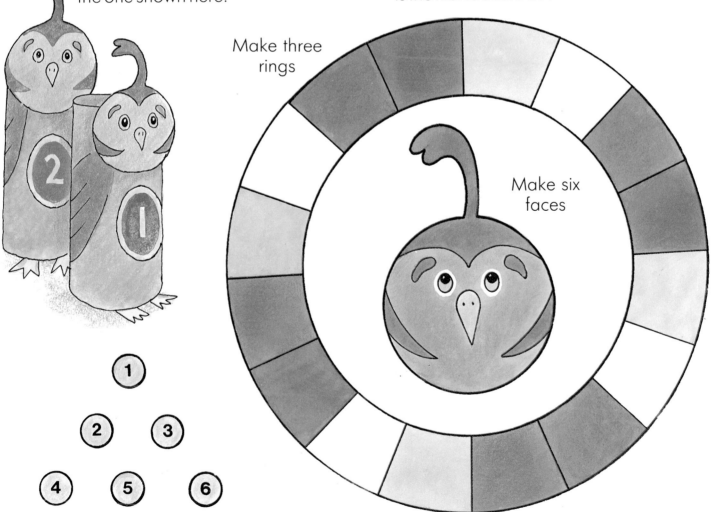

Make three rings

Make six faces

55

R is for rabbit

Make this family of finger puppets from pieces of felt. You will also need some stiff cardboard, tracing paper, glue, and scissors.

Lay your tracing paper over the rabbit outline, draw over it with pencil and cut out. This is your pattern. Now follow the pictures below.

1. Pin the pattern to the felt and draw around it twice. Cut out.

Pieces of felt glued on for eyes, etc.

2. Cut one of the shapes in half. Trace around the top half onto some cardboard.

3. Cut out the cardboard, and glue to the uncut rabbit. Glue the felt half on top.

4. Use a needle and thread to sew the lower halves together.

5. You could make clothes for the rabbits out of pieces of felt.

. . . and race

You don't have to be the fastest thing on two legs to win these crazy races!

How about racing with a book balanced on your head? . . .

. . . or running a somersault race . . .

. . . or racing in clothes that are much too big for you . . .

. . . or running backward?

S is for sand

Have you always suspected that there was more to sand than building castles? If so, try out some of these ideas the next time you're at the beach!

A mountain of sand can have channels for racing marbles down, or roads for cars, or fences made from sticks for a sandy zoo.

Remember—you should always wear a hat when you're out in hot sun.

Bury a friend in the sand up to his or her neck. You could shape the sand into a racing car or a moon rocket.

Think big! Try building a giant turtle coming out of the sea. Or make a whale, or a seal, or an imaginary monster. Shells, seaweeds, and sticks are good for decorating.

Draw a sunny seaside scene in the sand!

Dampen the sand with sea water, and use a stick to draw a tic-tac-toe board. Use seaweed and seashells as Xs and Os.

. . . snowman

Even if there is no snow outside, you can still build this snowman – and he won't melt away if it gets warm!

You will need: a jar, newspaper, glue, tape, absorbent cotton, paper, paints or felt-tip pens, some candy to fill the jar.

☆ Crumple a large sheet of newspaper into a ball, and tape firmly to the lid of the jar. Use more paper taped to the sides to make a fat snowman shape.

☆ Cover head and body with glue, and stick cotton all over. Fill the jar with candy.

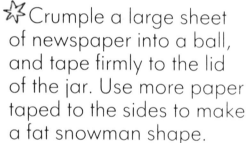

☆ Cut eyes, nose, mouth, and scarf from paper, and glue onto the snowman. Use part of a cardboard roll and two cardboard circles to make the snowman's hat. Glue together, paint, and glue to the snowman's head.

60

. . . and stars

Now you can stargaze without having to get out of bed! Cut out lots of shiny star and space shapes, and ask an adult to help you to put them on the walls and ceiling.

Find out about the stars and planets. Can you arrange the stars to form some of the well-known constellations (star patterns) you see in the sky at night?

T is for toad

Toads can play leapfrog too! Read the instructions on the next page to find out more about this waterlily hopping game for two players.

To play this game, you will need 10 green and 10 brown counters — use buttons or make them from cardboard.

HOW TO PLAY

1. One player puts 10 green counters in one corner; the other player puts 10 brown counters in the opposite corner.

2. The idea is to be the first to get all your counters to the opposite corner. You must move one counter only on each turn. You can move the counter to an empty square on either side, but *not* diagonally *(figure 1).*

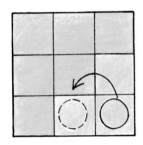 **1**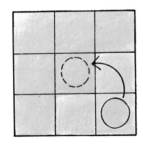

Right   *Wrong*

3. If there is another counter on the next square (your own counter *or* the other player's), you can hop over this — as long as there is an empty square on the other side *(figure 2).* If you find that you can hop over yet another counter when you land, you may do so in the same turn — and so on. The more hops you make on each turn, the better.

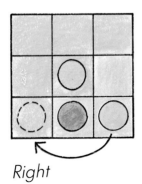 **2**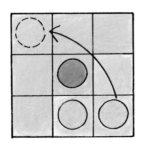

Right   *Wrong*

. . . and trail

Have you ever tried leaving a secret trail for someone to follow? All you need are a few sticks and stones, and a friend who knows what the secret signals mean. Here are a few to start you off — try making up lots more of your own.

Go straight on

Not this way

Hidden message

End of trail

Turn right

Not this way

U is for umbrella

As long as you take a hot bath and change clothes as soon as you go indoors, it can be great fun to play in the pouring rain! Never go out to play if there's any lightning.

Wear your waterproof coat and rubber boots, take your umbrella, and go splashing about in the puddles. Make up a rain dance, and go singing in the rain!

Don't let wet weather put you off — try playing your favorite games in the rain!

Have you ever tried skipping in the rain? Or playing leapsplash (a wet game of leapfrog)?

V is for vampire

This is a scary chase game for three or more players.

Make the vampire's outfit as shown below. The other players have three sticky red dots stuck to their clothes. When the vampire catches someone, he takes one of their dots. When a player loses all of his dots, he becomes a vampire too!

These fangs are made from orange peel.

Use black tissue paper or a black plastic garbage bag, and cut a batwing shape to fit the width of your arms. Pin this to your sleeves with safety pins.

. . . village

The models on these pages use matchboxes—but there's no reason why you can't make much bigger buildings using larger boxes. You will need lots of cardboard, paints, and glue as well.

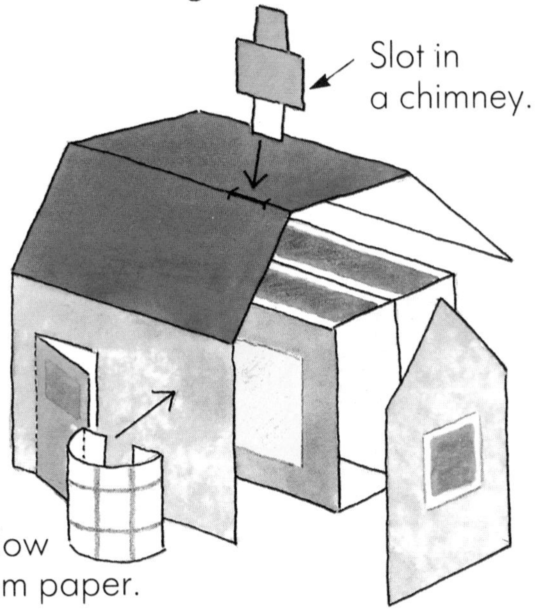

Slot in a chimney.

Separate roof

Bay window made from paper.

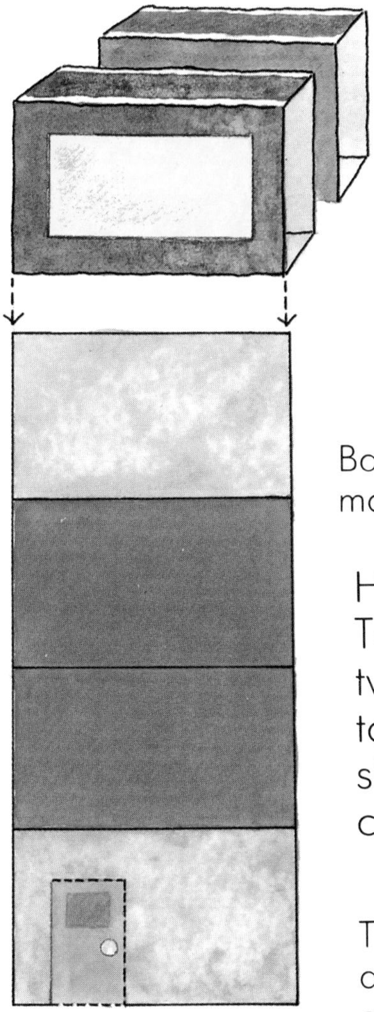

Doors can be cut to open out.

HOUSE
To make a house, glue two big matchboxes together. Use their shape as a guide for cutting out pieces of

This house also has a garage, made from a little matchbox.

cardboard to cover the front, sides, and roof (or make the roof separately, as shown above).

RAILROAD STATION

Give the roof a frilly edge like this. How about painting a station clock on the side? Raise the box on a little cardboard platform, and make a track from cardboard, too. The flowerpots are toothpaste-tube lids, and the plants are painted sponge.

STORES

Make a whole street of stores, with everything you would most like to buy painted in the window.

Hang signs on toothpicks.

TOWN HOUSE

Turn the matchboxes upright to make a house like this.

Put your village on a big sheet of cardboard. Paint in the roads, and make trees and bushes from painted pieces of sponge.

. . . and visitors

Here are three ways to make your guests feel special!

1. NAPKIN RING

☆ Glue a sheet of colored paper around an empty cardboard roll. Trim the edges, and cut the roll into rings. Cut circles from cardboard, and paint with a pattern or your visitors' names. Glue one to each ring.

2. PLACE CARD

☆ Fold a piece of thin cardboard about 5 x 4 inches (12 x 10 cm), in half. Unfold it, and copy the design shown here. Cut carefully around the hat shape, so that the hat stands up when the card is folded. Make a place card for each visitor.

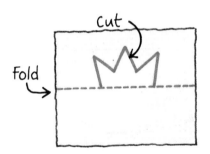

3. LACY PLACE MAT

☆ Fold a large paper napkin in half four times. Cut shapes out of the folded edges with scissors. Open up carefully.

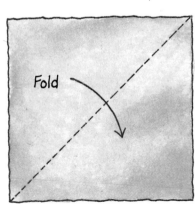

Open out

W is for washtime

Bathtime will never be the same again with this funny foam puppet! You will need some thin foam, scissors, a needle and thread, and a felt-tip pen.

Use the pen to draw around your hand onto the foam. Do this twice, and cut out. Sew the shapes together, leaving the bottom end open. Now turn the glove inside out. Use spare bits of foam for ears, eyes, legs, and arms.

. . . water

Another good thing about being outdoors is that you are usually allowed to get as wet as you like.

A leaky plastic bottle is just right for making a cooling shower. Leaky plastic cups are fun to play with, too . . . who can carry water the quickest from a full bucket of water to an empty one on the other side of the yard?

Empty dishwashing liquid bottles make good water pistols. Pile up some empty yogurt containers, and see how many you can knock over from five paces.

Make a shower

Yogurt containers

Water fights are fun!

Empty dishwashing liquid bottles make great water pistols.

. . . window

To make a "stained glass" window, you will need: some black cardboard or construction paper, colored tissue paper, glue, and scissors.

⭐ Draw a shape onto the black paper, using a light-colored pencil or chalk. Ask an adult to help you cut out the shape.

⭐ Glue pieces of tissue paper onto the back of the cardboard, so that the cut-out shape is completely covered.

Draw around the shape
of your window

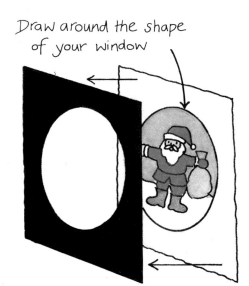

⭐ If you want to make a more detailed picture, first cut a simple shape out of black cardboard. Use it as a stencil to draw the same shape onto a piece of tracing paper.

Draw a design on the paper with black felt-tip pen. Turn the paper over, and fill in with colored felt-tip pens. Turn it back over again, and glue it into the black cardboard frame.

☆ Hang up your pictures in a window, so that light shines through the tissue or tracing paper.

. . . and wrapping paper

Presents look even more exciting if you make your own wrapping paper! You will need: some large sheets of plain paper, poster paints, a potato, a knife, newspaper (to cover your working surface).

✸ Clean the potato, and ask an adult to cut it in half. Draw a shape onto the cut surface with a pen, and ask an adult to cut away the edges so that the shape stands out.

✰ Mix some paint and water in a saucer. Dip the potato shape in the paint, and print patterns all over the plain paper. Leave to dry completely.

✸ Make matching gift tags and attach to the presents with ribbon.

74

X is for xylophone

Take six identical glass tumblers, and fill them up to the levels shown in the picture. Label the tumblers 1 to 6, so you don't get mixed up when you're giving your first concert!

Following the numbers below, see if your audience can recognize "Twinkle Twinkle, Little Star."

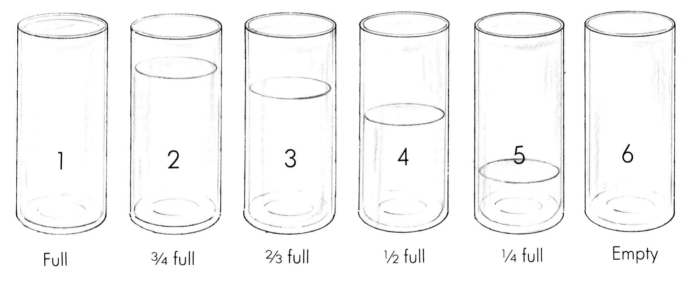

1	2	3	4	5	6
Full	¾ full	⅔ full	½ full	¼ full	Empty

① – ①   ⑤ – ⑤   ⑥ – ⑥   ⑤ | ④   ④   ③ – ③   ②   ②   ①
Twin – kle Twin – kle   lit – tle   star, | How   I   won – der   what   you   are.

⑤   ⑤ – ④   ④   ③   ③   ② | ⑤   ⑤   ④ – ④   ③   ③   ②
Up   a – bove   the   world   so   high | Like   a   dia – mond   in   the   sky.

① – ①   ⑤ – ⑤   ⑥ – ⑥   ⑤ | ④   ④   ③ – ③   ②   ②   ①
Twin – kle Twin – kle   lit – tle   star, | How   I   won – der   what   you   are.

Y is for yacht

To make colorful yachts for sailing on ponds or puddles, all you need are some corks, toothpicks, some thin cardboard, glue, and your poster paints.

First, glue four corks together, side by side. Now follow the picture instructions.

1. Cut the cardboard into squares as wide as the cork boats. Paint them brightly, and cut a tiny cross at the top and bottom.

2. Push toothpicks through the card squares. Glue them in place if they slip.

3. Push the toothpicks into the cork base.

. . and yawning

Did you know that yawns were catching?
Try it for yourself! Have a competition to
see who can hold out the longest without
joining in. Or try to trick an adult into
yawning without letting them know what
you are up to. The only danger is that you
might find yourself being sent to bed early!

Z is for zigzag

Choose two different pictures from a magazine – they should both be the same size. Now measure a piece of paper that is the same height and twice as long as the pictures.

1. Fold the paper and the pictures into zigzag pleats – each about 1 inch (3cm) wide.

3. Now fold up your zigzag picture. If you look at it from one side, you will see one of the pictures. If you look at it from the other side, the other picture will magically appear!

You can use zigzag pictures for unusual birthday cards and fun party invitations too!

Open them out, and divide the pictures into strips by cutting along the folded lines.

2. Take one of the pictures, and paste the first strip to the first pleat of the piece of paper. To the second pleat, paste the first strip of the other picture. Keep doing this until all the picture strips are in place.

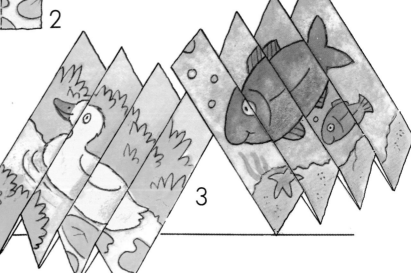

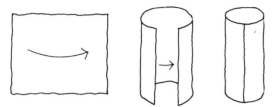

. . . and zoo

Did you know that you can make a whole zooful of animals from rolls of paper?

First, make lots of paper rolls like the ones shown here.

Roll up sheets of paper.

Put glue down one side, to make a roll shape.

LION
You will need the rolls and shapes shown below. Glue them together as shown in the picture, and make a tail from yarn.

Make a tail from yellow yarn.

Paint the pieces yellow.

PENGUINS
Each penguin is made from a paper roll, with a penguin shape and feet glued to the front.

Make a pool for the penguins from a shoebox lid. Paint the base blue and put some sand in the box.

Copy this shape.

Paint feet orange.

Paint roll black.

ZEBRA

You will need one long roll, one short roll pressed into an oval for the head, two big thin rolls for the legs, and two ears. Glue the rolls together, and cut slots in the head for the ears to fit into. You could use these kinds of rolls for making an elephant and a tiger, too.

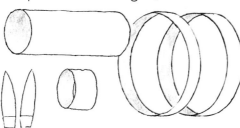

Paint rolls before threading.

SNAKE

You will need lots of little rolls. Thread them together through the middle using a needle and thread, so that the snake can wriggle. Give the front roll a little paper tongue.

PANDA

You will need the rolls and shapes shown below. Glue them together as shown.

Why not use brown-colored paper to make a bear in the same way?

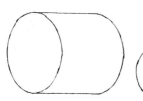

After you have made the zoo animals on these pages, try making up some of your own. When you have made the lion, how about making a lioness (just leave the mane off) and some little cubs? Remember, you can make all the models in smaller sizes for baby animals and in no time you can have a complete zoo of animal families made from paper!
